Architecture of the Off-Modern

Svetlana Boym

A copublication of the Buell Center / FORuM Project
and Princeton Architectural Press

This book is copublished by

The Temple Hoyne Buell Center
for the Study of American Architecture
1172 Amsterdam Avenue
Columbia University
New York, New York 10027
and
Princeton Architectural Press
37 East Seventh Street
New York, New York 10003

Visit our website at www.papress.com

© 2008 The Trustees of Columbia University
in the City of New York and Princeton
Architectural Press
Text © 2008 Svetlana Boym

All rights reserved.
First paperback edition, 2013
Printed and bound in China
16 15 14 13   4 3 2 1

No part of this book may be used or reproduced
in any manner without written permission from
the publisher, except in the context of reviews.

Every reasonable attempt has been made
to identify owners of copyright. Errors or
omissions will be corrected in subsequent
editions.

ISBN 978-1-61689-103-9

The Library of Congress has catalogued the
hardcover edition as follows:
Boym, Svetlana, 1959–
  Architecture of the off-modern.
80 p. : ill., (some col.) ; 23 cm. — (FORuM
project)
Includes bibliographical references.
ISBN 978-1-56898-778-1 (hardcover : alk. paper)
1. Architecture, Modern—20th century—
Philosophy. 2. Architecture and society. I.
Temple Hoyne Buell Center for the Study of
American Architecture. II. Title.
NA680.B69 2008
724'.6—dc22
                        2008005446

Architecture of the Off-Modern is the second
volume in a series of books related to the
FORuM Project, dedicated to exploring the
relationship of architectural form to politics
and urban life. FORuM is a program of The
Temple Hoyne Buell Center for the Study of
American Architecture at Columbia University.

Project conceptualization:
Joan Ockman and Pier Vittorio Aureli
Project coordination:
Sara Goldsmith and Diana Martinez

For The Temple Hoyne Buell Center
Series editor: Joan Ockman
Executive editor: Sara Goldsmith
Editorial assistant: Sharif Khalje
Copy editor: Stephanie Salomon
Designer: Dexter Sinister, New York

Special thanks to Salomon Frausto and
Richard Anderson

For Princeton Architectural Press
Production editor: Linda Lee

Special thanks to:
Sara Bader, Nicola Bednarek Brower,
Janet Behning, Fannie Bushin, Megan Carey,
Carina Cha, Andrea Chlad, Russell Fernandez,
Will Foster, Jan Haux, Diane Levinson,
Jennifer Lippert, Jacob Moore, Katharine
Myers, Margaret Rogalski, Elana Schlenker,
Dan Simon, Sara Stemen, Andrew Stepanian,
Paul Wagner, and Joseph Weston
of Princeton Architectural Press
—Kevin C. Lippert, publisher

Contents

4
Architecture of Adventure
and the Off-Modern

8
Tatlin's *Techne*
and Revolutionary Ruins

15
Architecture of Estrangement
and the Curve of Freedom

22
Architecture of Suspension
and Project-Poetics

28
Installation-Architecture
and Contemporary Ruinophilia

38
Notes and Credits

41
Illustrations

73
An Off-Modern Manifesto

Architecture of Adventure and the Off-Modern

1 Let us look at this strange cityscape: on the riverbanks of St. Petersburg the spires of the historic Peter and Paul Fortress compose a harmonic ensemble with Vladimir Tatlin's Monument to the Third International, known also as the Monument to the Liberation of Humanity or simply Tatlin's Tower. This is a picture-perfect view of my former hometown—St. Petersburg, Petrograd, Leningrad—not the way the city ever was, but the way it could have been. This is an image of an alternative modernity in which avant-garde projects transform the historical cityscape. It is up to us to decide whether this is a ruinscape or a utopian construction site, and whether we should think of it in the past imperfect or the future perfect.

What is at stake in dreaming of a conjectural history of modern architecture that never came to be? How does this oblique move challenge our understanding of art and technology, nostalgia and progress, and the future of the architectural imagination? To understand this, I will explore the architectural and philosophical metamorphosis of one of the icons of the Russian avant-garde, the legendary Tatlin's Tower, which will be the cornerstone of my genealogy of this alternative, "third-way" intellectual history of modernity. Rather than postmodern, I call it off-modern: it doesn't follow the logic of crisis and progress but rather involves an exploration of the side alleys and lateral potentialities of the project of critical modernity. I am tired of the "post," "neo," "avant," and "trans" of the charismatic post-criticism that tries to be desperately "in." There is another option: to be not "out," but "off," as in "off-stage," "off-key," "off-beat," and occasionally "off-color." It will help me explore alternative approaches to form and function, to the understanding of the relationship between artistic technique and technology, aesthetic practice and politics in the public sphere, ruinophilia and freedom.

Many theorists of the early twentieth century dreamed of "cheating" the straight narrative of progress and exploring third ways: zigzags, spirals, diagonals, the movements of the chess knight. Architectural shapes permeate philosophical discourse on modernity in the writings of Sigfried Kracauer, Walter Benjamin, Hannah Arendt, Georg Simmel, Franz Kafka, and others. Of particular importance will be one road not taken: that of Russian Formalist theory—Viktor Shklovsky's eccentric conception of the "knight's move," the lateral road of artistic renewal. Far from being a compromise, third-way thinking and the knight's move exemplify, in Shklovsky's view, the "tortured road of the brave," a path that estranges political, technological, and economic understandings of utility and function and suggests an interesting relationship between architectural and literary space.

In the early twentieth century architecture became a contested concept that some dreamed of throwing overboard from the "ship of modernity," to paraphrase Vladimir Mayakovsky and David Burlyuk's <u>A Slap in the Face of Public Taste</u>. The Surrealist heretic and mythographer Georges Bataille took a position "against architecture." Bataille preferred quasi-mythical spaces of violence like the slaughterhouse, made invisible in the modern "flabby world in which nothing fearful remains" and in which bored bourgeois are "reduced to eating cheese."[1] In his understanding, "architecture is the expression of the very being of societies" and of social hierarchies; hence it has to be stormed in revolutionary fashion, like the Bastille.

Sharing Bataille's heretical modernist zeal, I will be a "devil's advocate" for the opposite. It is precisely because architecture is a material expression of society that it needs to be taken into account and examined in terms of what Kracauer called our "existential topography" or what I call cultural mnemotics. Architecture in this understanding is not architectonics; it does not give a system or a superstructure to the world of concepts, but rather a texture. Architecture has the potential to be a form of *poiesis*—making that doesn't merely reify hierarchies, but commemorates human labor and artifice, exceeds its own immediate function, and contributes to the making of world culture.[2] There has always been a double movement between architectural and philosophical reflection.

I am interested not in symbolic form in architecture, but rather in the narrative and spatial configuration of third-way thinking that includes architecture, theory, modernist fiction, philosophy, and other forms of eccentric and experimental theoretical storytelling, which often find themselves in the cracks between intellectual genres, systems of thought, and disciplines. This form of thought is not about system-building but rather about life and art as project and adventure. Literature and philosophy provide many models of potential spaces—not utopias, but an imaginary topography that can offer models for the future. Adventure provides a possibility for reverse mimesis— instead of imitating nature, intense imagination offers an architecture of the future. Literature and philosophy can be forms of "paper architecture."

The architecture of the off-modern, in my understanding, is the architecture of adventure. Adventure literally refers to something that is about to happen, *à venir*. But instead of opening up into some catastrophic or messianic future, it leads rather into invisible temporal dimensions of the present. One of the most interesting thinkers of third terms in the early twentieth century, Georg Simmel, proposed a phenomenology of adventure that both interrupts the flow of our everyday life and crystallizes its inner core.[3] Adventure is a third "something," neither an external incident nor an internal system. In adventure we "forcibly pull the world into ourselves," like conquerors, but at the same time allow a "complete self-abandonment to the powers and accidents of the world which can delight us and destroy us."[4]

The architecture of adventure is the architecture of thresholds, liminal spaces, porosity, doors, bridges, and windows. It is not about experiences of the sublime, but of the liminal. Adventure is like "a stranger's body" that foregrounds that which is most intimate: "It is a foreign body in our existence which is yet somehow connected with the center; the outside, if only by a long and unfamiliar detour, is formally an aspect of the inside."[5] Adventure has the shape of a Möbius strip, and an inside-out structure of imagination that comes from inside but allows human beings to embrace the cosmos beyond their immediate experience. The temporality of adventure mirrors its spatial structure. Adventure is time out of time; while bounded by its beginning and ending, it reveals the limitless force and potential of life. The adventurer "burns bridges" and travels with the certainty of a sleepwalker into the mist, yet she never lands on the other side. She pushes "life beyond the threshold of its temporal boundaries," but this "beyond" is never beyond this-worldliness. Neither transcendence nor transgression, it is a potentiality, an encounter with the incalculable that forces us to change life's calculus. In other words, in response to the Weberian disenchantment of the modern world enforced by bureaucratic regimes of states and corporations, adventure promises re-enchantment in a minor existential key. Adventure is a kind of profane illumination, not a rapture; it pushes human possibilities but does not transgress them.

This essay will take up historical, phenomenological, and artistic aspects of the architecture of the off-modern. It is important, in my view, not to shy away from an actual history of the avant-garde that goes beyond Western European and American contexts and, learning from this history, to expand the conception of "architecture" by including its manifestations in literary, cinematic, and theoretical accounts of the time. First, I will suggest an alternative historical genealogy of avant-garde experimentation, one that neither "ends" in the 1930s or the 1970s nor simply develops into Socialist Realism or modernist functionalism, but rather opens toward an off-centered horizon of experimentation that remains largely unexplored. Second, I will look at the architecture of adventure in its temporal and spatial dimensions and examine the conception of *techne* as a mediation between art and technology and of *ostranenie* (estrangement) as a mediation between aesthetic and political realms, important for third-way thinking and an art of dissent. Third, I will explore the small-scale architecture of models and projects, not as a theater of failure, dysfunction, and purposelessness, but as an off-beat laboratory of imagination that builds bridges between architecture, conceptual installation, and media art. The off-modern perspective challenges the concept of the "originality of the avant-garde" elaborated by Rosalind Krauss as well as the idea of the continuity of the utopian vision between the avant-garde and Socialist Realism put forward by Boris Groys.[6] Instead, it reveals the avant-garde's internal diversity, its singularities and eccentricities, which proved to be as historically relevant and persistent as its visionary elements and collective utopianism.

There are no elements of style or form that are by definition "freer" than others. We know that the architecture of authoritarian and totalitarian states happily appropriated and compromised every possible style—from pyramids, ziggurats, classical porticos, and Roman coliseums to Art Deco, modernist functionalism, and postmodernism. My approach to architecture is neither that of the philosopher René Descartes, who proposed the (foundationalist) notion of a single architect making his master design of the world, nor that of Jacques Derrida, who advanced a radically anti-foundationalist understanding of an "architecture to come" (*architecture à venir*). I am interested not in anti-architecture, but in off-architecture, or occasionally in an-architecture (to use the artist Gordon Matta-Clark's concept), which marks the mnemotic commonplaces of different kinds of collective human artifice. Both ruins and construction sites provide perfect metaphors for architecture's potentials. In Eastern Europe there was a well-established tradition of paper architecture—an architecture of radical projects done during the "era of stagnation" that were meant for architectural competitions but never built. They were architecturally adventurous even if barely functional. This kind of architecture is not immaterial; rather it redefines the relationship between materiality and virtuality in the broadest sense of the word "virtual," ranging from a virtuality of imagination to one of technology.

Tatlin's *Techne* and Revolutionary Ruins

Vladimir Tatlin's Monument to the Third International (1919–25) was an adventurous revolutionary experiment—although, contrary to conventional wisdom, the notions of "adventure," "revolution," and "experiment" it embodied were frequently contradictory, if not mutually exclusive. Leon Trotsky praised Tatlin's formal innovation in "discarding from his project national styles, allegorical sculpture, modeled monograms, flourishes and tails" but commented that Tatlin's Tower, like the Eiffel Tower, alienates viewers with its purposelessness. "The props and the piles which are to support the glass cylinder and the pyramid—and they are there for no other purpose— are so cumbersome and heavy that they look like unremoved scaffolding," wrote Trotsky.[7] While acutely perceptive about the contradictions of art and life, Trotsky underestimated the purpose of "purposelessness" in postrevolutionary times. The tower became a kind of scaffolding for a future architecture that lays bare many architectural functions, including the functions of experimental imagination and of project-making that may or may not result in an actual building.

The Monument to the Third International was meant to be radically anti-monumental. As a manifesto of the architectural revolution, Tatlin's Tower challenged both the "bourgeois" Eiffel Tower and the American Statue of Liberty. Constructed of iron and glass, it consisted of three rotating glass volumes: a cube, a pyramid, and a cylinder. The cube was supposed to house the Soviet of the People's Commissars of the World (Sovnarkom) and turn at the rate of one revolution a year; the pyramid, intended for the executive and administrative committees of the Third International, would rotate once a month; and the cylinder, a center for information and propaganda, would complete one revolution daily. Radio waves would extend the tower into the sky, and the typographic workshops on the third floor would project the motto of the day out onto the clouds. In fact, the tower embodied many explicit and implicit meanings of the word "revolution." The word, which came from scientific discourse, originally meant repetition and rotation. Only in the seventeenth century did it begin to signify its opposite: a breakthrough, an unrepeatable event. The tower's program reflects upon the ambivalent relationship between art and science, revolution and repetition. Shaped as a spiral, a favorite

Marxist-Hegelian form, the tower culminated in a radical opening on top, suggesting unfinalizability, not synthesis. In fact, the tower commemorated the short-lived utopia of the permanent artistic revolution. Tatlin was one of that revolution's leaders. He declared that the revolution began not in 1917 but in 1914 with an artistic transformation; political revolution followed in the steps of the artistic one, mostly unfaithfully.

A contemporary of Tatlin, the well-known theorist of Constructivism Nikolai Punin, described the monument as the anti-ruin *par excellence*. In his view, Tatlin's revolutionary architecture reduced to ashes the classical and Renaissance traditions. The "charred ruins of Europe are now being cleared," he wrote.[8] In the design of the tower, Tatlin sabotaged the perfect verticality of the Eiffel Tower by choosing the form of a spiral and leaning it to one side. At the same time, uncannily, Tatlin's monument was also not free of the charm of the ruin. In its attempt to be the anti-Eiffel Tower, it started to resemble the leaning Tower of Pisa, or even the Tower of Babel.

El Lissitzky praised Tatlin's Tower for its "synthesis between the technical and the artistic," between old and new forms: "Here the Sargon Pyramid at Khosabad was actually recreated in a new material with a new content."[9] The project in Khosabad was, in fact, a ziggurat, a pyramidal structure with a flat top, which most likely corresponded to the mythical shape of the Tower of Babel, which in turn resembled the ziggurat at Babylon, called Etemenanki.[10] Thus, in its attempt to be the anti-Eiffel Tower, Tatlin's Tower harked back to the Tower of Babel, an unfinished utopian monument turned mythical ruin. Moreover, in the case of the Tower of Babel, the tale of architectural utopia and its ruination is mirrored by the related parable about language. The Tower of Babel, as may be recalled, was built to ensure perfect communication with God. Its failure ensured the survival of art. Since then, every builder of a tower has dreamed of touching the sky, and, of course, the gesture has remained forever asymptotal.

Perhaps every functional modern tower evokes the mythic malfunctioning of this original dream of total communication. Roland Barthes wrote that while Gustave Eiffel himself saw his tower "in the form of a serious object, rational, useful, men return it to him in the form of a great baroque dream which quite naturally touches on the borders of the irrational."[11] Barthes's poetic commemoration of the uselessness of the Eiffel Tower could easily apply to its Soviet rival as well. Much visionary architecture, in Barthes's view, embodies a profound double movement; it is always "a dream and a function, an expression of a utopia and instrument of a convenience." Barthes saw the Eiffel Tower as an "empty" memorial that contained nothing, but from whose top you could see the world. It became an optical device for a vision of modernity. Tatlin's Tower played a similar role: as an observatory for the palimpsest of revolutionary panoramas that included ruins and construction sites alike.

Tatlin's Tower—unlike the Eiffel Tower—failed to be realized not merely because of engineering problems and concerns about feasibility. It was both behind and ahead of its time. Clashing with the postrevolutionary architectural trends, its model nevertheless was exhibited and used during the parades celebrating the October Revolution. Thus it existed as an incomplete theatrical set, a part of official street theater, not gigantic but human-scale, a testimony to revolutionary transience.

Tatlin's Tower was also "translated" into Western languages in the Babelian fashion: much was lost in translation. In 1920, articles about the tower appeared in the Munich art magazine <u>Der Ararat</u> and caught the attention of the emerging Dadaists. "Art is dead," declared the Dadaists. "Long live the machine art of Tatlin!"[12] Yet to some extent, the Dadaists' celebration of the death of art by way of Tatlin's spiral "guillotine" was an act of cultural mistranslation and reflected a common Western misconception about the Russian avant-garde. By no means was Tatlin a proponent of machine-assisted artistic suicide, especially not at the time of the revolution, when the "death of art" was more than a metaphor. Instead, Tatlin argued against the "tyranny of forms born by technology without the participation of artists." Lissitzky wrote that Tatlin's greatest achievement lay in the artistic mastery of the materials and techniques, quite independent of the "rational and scientific methods of technology."[13] Tatlin accomplished his task without having any specific technical knowledge of construction and without proper architectural drawings, thus proving Lissitzky's assumption. Tatlin's Tower, in Lissitzky's view, was "an open building" that offered extension in space and time by not "shutting the building between the walls," revealing "an open skeleton" of functional parts and by introducing rotation in time. Tatlin's own slogans, "Art into life" and "Art into technology," do not, in fact, suggest putting art in the service of life or technology, nor putting life in the service of political or social revolution. Rather, they propose to revolutionize technology and society by opening horizons of imagination and moving beyond mechanistic clichés. In this case, the two meanings of the word *techne*—that of art and that of technical craft—continuously duel with one another: art estranges technology, while new technology provides inspiration for artistic experimentation.[14] Tatlin's Tower came into being as a theatrical fragment and an unfinished model of paper architecture, a utopian scaffolding that resembled a future ruin.

9–11 Tatlin's architectural and technological projects belong to the realm of adventure rather than functionalism. What is interesting about Tatlin is that after the tower he continued to think about the issue of technique as a third way between art and technology. Most radically this is demonstrated in his project "Letatlin" (a neologism that combines the Russian verb "to fly"—*letat*—with his own name) of the late 1920s and early 1930s. If Tatlin's Tower was a dream of the perfect collective of the Third International, Letatlin was an individual flying vehicle. A biomorphic structure, it resembled at once a flying bicycle *à la* Duchamp and the firebird of Russian fairytales. Tatlin was briefly employed by the Soviet aviation industry, which wanted him to create a perfect spy plane; instead, he made a vehicle for a belated, avant-garde Icarus that could not fly—not in a literal sense at least. Thus, Letatlin is more about aesthetic and existential adventure than about the technological progress of rocket science.[15] Both projects, the flying machine and the tower, belong to a very different history of technology, an enchanted technology, founded on charisma as much as calculus, linked to premodern myths as well as to modern science. Yet neither are they altogether alien to the history of Soviet cosmonautics; in the Soviet exploration of the cosmos, science merged with science fiction, and ideology occasionally sounded like poetry. The tower resembles the ruin of a mythical space station from which Letatlins could fly off into the sky.

Tatlin's artistic life from the mid-1920s to the mid-1930s is rich in contradictions, refracting his time. He designed the coffin for Russia's revolutionary poet Vladimir Mayakovsky, who committed suicide in 1930. In 1934, the Soviet Security Agency (OGPU), the predecessor to the KGB, invited him together with other artists to observe the construction of the Belomor Canal, one of the early sites of Stalin's slave labor. At the exhibition Artists of Russia, of 1933, his works were shown in a small hall dedicated to "Formalist excesses" (a successful predecessor to the "Degenerate Art" exhibition in Germany). The official Soviet critics proclaimed that Tatlin's works demonstrated "the natural death of formal experiments in art" and declared Tatlin to be "no artist whatsoever" (*nikakoi xudozhnik*).[16]

What do artists do when they outlive their cultural relevance? In the Soviet case we know very little about the last fifteen years of work of the founders of the visual avant-garde, including Tatlin, who died in 1953. What can an avant-garde artist make after his officially declared death? Tatlin's "postmortem" work consists—literally—of *natures mortes*, and of desolate rural landscapes painted on backdrops of Socialist Realist theater productions, mostly done in a brown and gray palette. In my view, the untimeliness of Tatlin's late still lifes and landscapes speaks obliquely of their time—the time of purges and war. While figurative, these works hardly reflect the optimistic tone of Socialist Realist art, suggesting instead another existential perspective. *Nature morte* is one of the ancient genres of world painting, surviving historical cataclysms and artistic and social revolutions. Still lifes are reminders of the other, nonrevolutionary rhythms of everyday life. They preserve the dream of home, of domesticated nature, and of a long-standing artistic tradition. Tatlin's still lifes look like *mementi mori*, foregrounding the fragility of even the most frugal domesticity.¹⁷ There is a subtle tension between these ahistorical still lifes and the dates they were painted: years of Stalin's purges right after World War II. Moreover, the closer we look at Tatlin's still lifes, the more they appear to be exercises in double vision, but not in the conventional sense of political double-speak. Rather there is a tension between the figurative flowers and the abstract background. In the foreground are the sparse still lifes, and in the background, the thickly painted planes from which Tatlin's famous counter-reliefs once sprung. Tatlin's biomorphic revolutionary Icaruses, the Letatlins, abandoned these unspectacular and belated stage sets. Tatlin's late works resemble desolate "natural settings" in which the projects of the avant-garde turned into ruins of the revolution.

In fact, the architectural adventures of Tatlin's Tower have developed in two directions—toward restorative and toward reflective nostalgia. The emblematic idea of the revolutionary building *par excellence* was adopted by Stalin, and he proposed to build the ultimate one—the Palace of the Soviets—so as to supplant the dream of the Third International. According to Stalin's plan, the colossus of a new era—416 meters high, terraced, colonnaded, and adorned with sculptures by the architect Boris Iofan—was not only to succeed the cathedral with a shrine to victorious atheism, but it was to be the Soviet response to the Statue of Liberty and the Empire State Building. Iofan proudly declared that the Palace of the Soviets would be eight meters taller than the Empire State Building. Crowned with a 6,000-ton statue of Lenin with an outstretched hand showing the enlightened path to mankind, it was criticized by Vyacheslav Molotov, who thought it absurd that the Soviet people would not be able to look into Lenin's eyes, but Stalin assured him this would not be a problem. The Palace of Soviets made the dynamic spiral static, immobilized the Hegelian dialectics into an imperial synthesis, and placed the statue of Lenin precisely where Tatlin's sculpture had featured an openness and defiance of representation.¹⁸

On the other hand, Tatlin's Tower became a twentieth-century artistic myth and an inspiration for the unofficial art of the postwar era, which was nostalgic for the boldness of the revolutionary imagination, not for the revolution itself. Artistic and social revolutions ended up like thesis and antithesis. In the end, the unbuilt monuments to collective utopia turned into mementos of individual dreams and places of dissent.

So Tatlin's Tower was not destined to exist in the open space of the city. Instead it acquired a second life in many models built around the world since the 1960s. One of the most faithful replicas was reconstructed on the floor of the mosaic factory where Tatlin worked. It was carried out between 1986 and 1991 by a group of young Russian architects and designers who performed a meticulous analysis of Tatlin's sketches and 1920s photographs. Tatlin, faithful to avant-garde technique, left no professional architectural drawings of the project, making space for unpredictability and imagination. This recent Russian tribute to Tatlin coincided with the end of the Soviet Union and the beginning of perestroika and glasnost—which did not last long. Never realized as a radical revolutionary monument, the tower came into material existence as a piece of "artistic heritage."

Architecture of Estrangement and the Curve of Freedom

From the very beginning, Tatlin's Tower engendered its double— a discursive monument almost as prominent as its architectural original. Shklovsky was one of the few contemporaries who appreciated the tower's unconventional architecture, which for him was an architecture of estrangement. Its temporal vectors pointed toward the past and the future, toward "the iron age of Ovid" and the "age of construction cranes, beautiful like wise Martians."[19] The construction cranes, the wise Martians, and the exiled poet Ovid all collaborated in the making of the tower. Shklovsky ends his essay about the tower by laying bare its unconventional materials: "The monument is made of iron and glass and revolution."[20] The air of the revolution functioned as the project's immaterial glue. Thus at the origins of modernist functionalism in architecture was the poetic function.

Describing the "semantics" of the tower, Shklovsky speaks of poetry: "The word in poetry is not merely a word, it drags with it dozens of associations. This work is filled with them like the Petersburg air in the winter whirlwind."[21]

Hence the tower was not merely an engineering failure but an exemplary case study of Constructivist architecture. Architecture was imagined as "archi-art," as a framework for a worldview and a carcass for futuristic dreams. This made it both more and less than architecture in the sense of a built environment. Revolutionary architecture offered scenography for future experimentation and embodied allegories of the revolution. Many significant examples of this "archi-art" were not built monuments, but rather dreamed environments or unintentional memorials. Shklovsky describes his own ludic ruin/construction site, laying a foundation for the subversive practice of estrangement.

It is little known that Shklovsky was the first to describe the Soviet version of the Statue of Liberty. In his collection of essays and sketches <u>The Knight's Move</u> (1919–21), written in Petrograd, Moscow, and Berlin, Shklovsky offered his readers a parable about the metamorphosis of historical monuments that functions as a strange alibi for not telling "the whole truth," or even "a quarter of the truth," as he puts it, about the situation in postrevolutionary Russia. In 1918 in Petrograd the monument to Tsar Alexander III was covered up by a cardboard stall with all kinds of slogans celebrating liberty, art, and revolution.[22] The "Monument to Liberty" was one of those transient nonrepresentational monuments that exemplified early postrevolutionary "visual propaganda" before the granite megalomania of the Stalinist period. This is how Shklovsky introduces the story:

> No, not the truth. Not the whole truth. Not even a quarter of the truth. I do not dare to speak and awaken my soul. I put it to sleep and covered it with a book, so that it would not hear anything…
>
> There is a tombstone by the Nicholas Station. A clay horse stands with its feet planted apart, supporting the clay backside of a clay boss…. They are covered by the wooden stall of the "Monument to Liberty" with four tall masts jutting from the corners. Street kids

peddle cigarettes, and when militia men with guns come to catch them and take them away to the juvenile detention home, where their souls can be saved, the boys shout scram! and whistle professionally, scatter, run toward the Monument to Liberty.

Then they take shelter and wait in that strange place—in the emptiness beneath the boards between the tsar and the revolution.[23]

In Shklovsky's description, the monument to the tsar is not yet destroyed and the monument to liberty is not entirely completed. A double political symbol turns into a lively and ambivalent urban site inhabited by insubordinate Petrograd street kids in an unpredictable manner. (Shklovsky calls them "Petrograd gavroches," making an explicit allusion to the French Revolution and its fictional representations.) In this description, the monument acquires an interior; a public site becomes a hiding place. Identifying his viewpoint with the dangerous game of the street kids hiding "between the tsar and the revolution," Shklovsky is looking for a third way, for a transitory and playful architecture of freedom.[24] He performs a double estrangement, defamiliarizing both the authority of the tsar and the liberation theology of the revolution. "Third way" here suggests a spatial and a temporal paradox. The monument caught in the moment of historical transformation embodies what Walter Benjamin called the "dialectic at a standstill." The first Soviet statue of liberty was at once a ruin and a construction site; it occupied a gap between the past and the future in which various versions of Russian history would coexist and clash.

The ambivalence of Shklovsky's parable betrays the precariousness of the writer's own political situation. The founder of Formalist theory, Shklovsky had an adventurous albeit brief political career. He took part in World War I and was awarded a Georgian Cross for outstanding bravery. Severely wounded twice, with seventeen pieces of shrapnel in his body, he was operated on in a military hospital and, according to his own recollection, tried to recite the poetry of Velimir Khlebnikov to the surgeon in order to distract himself from the pain. Though a supporter of the February Revolution, he did not initially embrace the events of October 1917. In fact, in 1918

Shklovsky joined the Socialist Revolutionary Party, which voted against the Bolshevik dispersal of the Constitutional Assembly; later he became one of the organizers of an anti-Bolshevik coup. Shklovsky was an advocate of democratic freedoms (just like the writer Maxim Gorky at that time), and in much of his postrevolutionary autobiographical writing the discourse on public freedom is present between the lines of his texts, often through references to the French Revolution and theories of the social contract. This was his own version of "socialism with a human face," to apply an anachronistic description. Threatened with arrest and possible execution, Shklovsky crossed the border on the frozen Gulf of Finland and eventually found himself in Berlin. <u>The Knight's Move</u> was written as the writer reflected on whether he should return from exile, back to Russia where his wife was being held hostage. The parable about the Monument to Liberty becomes an allegory of the transformation of the revolution and its many lost opportunities.

    Shklovsky's Monument to Liberty is thus a monument to his favorite device of *ostranenie*, or estrangement, which also undergoes some postrevolutionary transformations and "emigrates" from the text into life. Let us remember that Shklovsky coined the neologism *ostranenie* in his early essay "Art as Technique" to suggest both distancing (dislocating, *dépaysement*) and making strange.[25] *Stran* is the root of the Russian word for country, *strana*, and also of the word for strange, *strannyi*, its Latin and Slavic roots superimposed upon one another, creating a wealth of poetic associations and false etymologies. It is not by chance that Shklovsky refers to Aristotle's observation that poetic language is always to some degree a foreign language. Foreignness here is of a poetic and productive kind, enticing rather than alienating. From the very beginning, Shklovsky's *ostranenie* is defined differently from alienation, the latter usually translated by the Russian term *otchuzhdenie*. Shklovsky's theory of estrangement was intended in opposition to the economic and utilitarian discourse of efficiency and useful expenditure. The device of estrangement places emphasis on the process rather than the product of art, on retardation and deferral of *dénouement*, on cognitive ambivalence and play. By making things strange, the artist does not simply displace them from an everyday context into an artistic framework; he also helps to "return sensation" to life itself, to reinvent the world, to allow the observer to experience it anew. Estrangement is what makes art artistic; but by the same token, it makes life lively, or worth living.

In Shklovsky's view, estrangement is an exercise of wonder, of thinking of the world as a question, not as a staging of a grand answer. Thus, estrangement lays bare the boundaries between art and life but never pretends to abolish or blur them. It does not facilitate a seamless translation of life into art, nor the wholesale aestheticization of politics. Art is only meaningful when it is not entirely in the service of real life or *realpolitik*, and when its strangeness and distinctiveness are preserved. Thus the device of estrangement can both define and defy the autonomy of art.

Such an understanding of estrangement is different from both Hegelian and Marxist notions of alienation. Artistic estrangement is not to be cured by incorporation, synthesis, or belonging. In contrast to the Marxist notion of freedom that consists in overcoming alienation, Shklovskian estrangement is in itself a form of limited freedom endangered by all kinds of modern teleologies. It is not about building systems but about thinking of life and art as a continuous project, not a product.[26] Estrangement is more than a gesture and a technique; it delimits a certain kind of utopian architecture that exists in the emptiness "between the tsar and the revolution." Shklovsky's own imagined architecture of freedom came to be represented not by the functionalism of modernist architecture, but by the poetic function shaped by the knight's move or by Lobachevskian parallels. Like his contemporaries, Shklovsky was fascinated by modern science, from Einstein's theory of relativity to Nikolai Lobachevsky's non-Euclidean geometry. Shklovsky's <u>The Knight's Move</u> opens with a kind of Baroque emblem—a chessboard with the serpentine diagonal of the knight's move across the gridded space, and the following statement:

> There are many reasons for the strangeness of the knight's move, and the most important reason is the conventionality of art. I write about the conventionality of art. The second reason is that the knight is unfree, he moves sideways because the straight road is banned to him ...
>
> In Russia everything is so contradictory that we all became witty unwillingly.... Our torturous road is the road of the brave, but what else can we do when we have two eyes and see more than honest pawns or dutifully single-minded kings?[27]

The knight's serpentine road allows the "brave" literary thinker to see beyond appearances and to develop an alternative project, one that involves a playful public realm. But this kind of architecture of freedom and unofficial estrangement would not survive for long in the Soviet Union. Shklovsky was accused of Formalist baroque, confusion of revolutions, neo-Kantianism, bourgeois third-way thinking, "neutralization of the ideological front," and other vices. In her diary of 1927, Lydia Ginsburg, the literary critic and younger disciple of Shklovsky and his colleague Yuri Tynianov, observed: "The merry times of laying bare the device have passed (leaving us a real writer —Shklovsky). Now is the time when one has to hide the device as far as one can."[28] The practice of aesthetic estrangement became politically suspect by the late 1920s; by 1930, it turned into an intellectual crime. In spite of continuous attacks on his work and official demands for narrative and ideological coherence, however, the devices Shklovsky used in his texts remained almost unchanged as he continued to speak the Aesopian language of the nearly extinct "Formalist guild" until his death in 1984. Miraculously surviving various campaigns against him, Shklovsky remained a great theorist-storyteller like Walter Benjamin, who likewise spoke in elaborate parables, full of self-contradiction, in a unique style of "Formalist baroque." In the end, the Formalist critic was not practicing literary science but narrating the end of the Soviet literary public sphere.

Shklovsky wrote in 1926 that the Soviet writer of the 1920s had two choices: to write for the desk drawer or to write on state demand. "There is no third alternative. Yet that is precisely the one that must be chosen."²⁹ The writer, Shklovsky suggests, is not like a streetcar that can run on two parallel rails on a prescribed path. But I see a "parallelism" between Shklovsky's architecture of estrangement and Hannah Arendt's search for an unpredictable third way of freedom. Arendt describes freedom as something "fundamentally strange" that pushes people beyond the "routinization and automatization of modern life."³⁰ Just as *ostranenie* for Shklovsky was never estrangement from the world but rather an estrangement for the sake of the world's renewal, so Arendt imagines freedom's unpredictable architecture with the help of literature, philosophy, and theater, dreaming of asymptotic curves and diagonals. Her essay "What Is Freedom?" begins with a reflection on hopelessness: "To raise the question, what is freedom? seems to be a hopeless enterprise."³¹ To the philosopher it appears as impossible to conceive of freedom or its opposite as it is to realize the notion of a squared circle. The asymptotal space between the square and the circle might be the best representation of human freedom. This imaginary architectural space in Arendt's essays projects the philosopher into a daring diagonal of liminal freedom: Arendt's version of Shklovsky's knight's move.

Tracing the genealogy of the idea of freedom in the West, Arendt finds its origins in the *polis*, in public space—not in the inner citadel of one's psyche nor in the politics of the state. The Stoic conception of inner freedom was developed in an age of empire, not surprisingly. Stoic philosophers also used architectural metaphors, speaking about the "inner *polis*." Public freedom, unlike liberation, cannot exist without a public space and democratic institutions; yet the experience of freedom is not limited to procedural democracy. Freedom for Arendt is akin to a performance on a public stage—a performance that needs a common language but also a degree of incalculability, luck, chance, hope, surprise, wonder. Arendt uses aesthetic metaphors to speak about freedom: freedom is a kind of art, yet its model is not the plastic but the performing arts. Importantly, Arendt's conception of the art of freedom is also entirely different from the notion of a "total work" of politics. It entails a non-Wagnerian conception of aesthetic practice that focuses on process and not product. To think and experience the world aesthetically does not mean to make an authorial masterwork. Quite the contrary: an Arendtian aesthetic practice that engages acting, thinking, and judging would lay bare any attempt at creating a charismatic new myth. Arendt's philosophy of freedom mediates between existential, political, and aesthetic dimensions.

The Arendtian conception of the public realm is also radically different from that of Carl Schmitt, who has a binary and quasi-theological model of friend-and-foe agonism that turns the public space into an illusory disguise for primary power struggles. Arendt, more like Shklovsky, thinks of freedom and public architecture not in "dyadic" but in triadic forms.[32] Freedom is porous and open, not sovereign; the space of freedom is agnostic, not agonistic. While Arendt is interested in agonism, she views violence as the limit of the political. She has no appreciation for the mythical romanticism and charismatic theologies of sacrifice.

To sum up, it is possible to distinguish two kinds of estrangement. I would call them estrangement *from* the world and estrangement *for* the world. Estrangement from the world has its origins in the Stoic concept of inner freedom, as well as in Romantic subjectivity and introspection. Estrangement for the world is an acknowledgment of plurality, of the web of human interactions, of critical judgment and freedom. For both Shklovsky and Arendt, the architecture of freedom is always a space of unfinalizability and experimentation that depends on cultural forms and political institutions but is not entirely circumscribed by them. Freedom is a project of co-creation, not a finished product or a conspicuously coherent logical system of thought, and that's what brings it close to an off-modern poetics.

Architecture of Suspension
and Project-Poetics

For many of Tatlin's contemporaries, fellow avant-garde artists and writers, his tower exemplified the work of estrangement.

The very fact that it was known primarily as a model or a project rather than a realized building reflected the possibilities and contradictions of the time. Thus, instead of speculating on the technical feasibility of its construction, a subject that has preoccupied many architects and others over the years, it is more productive to think about the tower's actual history as a model and a project that opened up a new dimension of this intermediary and transitional architecture, which also may be called an architecture of possibility. "Project," in the case of the tower, was not an end in itself, but neither was it an impasse. It was a crucible of possibilities and inspirations, not a utilitarian blueprint. Projects and models play a key part in the alternative history of the "off-modern." In the context of the Russian avant-garde, artists and architects were frequently also writers. Their multifaceted production, often made "for the drawers" at a time when it was becoming increasingly difficult to build and publish, amounted to a different kind of a "total work," one that was necessarily fragmented and came to constitute an avant-garde art of dissent.

Kazimir Malevich, whose late work still provokes much debate about figuration, abstraction, and the politics of representation, gives us an insight into the artistic and political situation of the 1920s in his writings, which are often less enigmatic than his late paintings. In 1929 Malevich wrote retrospectively about what he saw as a synthesis of sculpture and architecture in Tatlin's work: "For him the most important thing was not a combination of the utilitarian functions but the union of the artistic side with the material, plus function .... The material was always selected according to a feeling of an artistic impression, not in relation to utility."[33] What is at stake here is not the opposition between the artistic and the utilitarian, but rather the insistence on a nonagonistic relationship between the two. Partly, this insistence is due to the megalomaniac role of art in Russian culture. Art in Russia (first literature and later the visual arts) was often perceived as a form of philosophy, politics, and religion, or even, in the words of Alexander Solzhenitsyn, a "second government." The radical imagination of the Russian avant-garde was frequently subsumed under the category of "utopia," which added to it an exotic flavor cherished by both Russian and Western theorists. In fact, there was greater diversity within the avant-garde, and in my view, the radicalism of the avant-garde imagination resides precisely in its atopian or heterotopian quality.

Soviet Russia was a land of great projections by the West. These had more to do with Western dreams than realities. For American and Western European Conceptual art, Tatlin, like Duchamp, was a major figure, but since very little was known about him, he became, in the words of Stephen Bann, "a vacuum" into which the engagement and interest of contemporary Western onlookers were attracted.[34] More valuable is to learn from Tatlin's particular Soviet history, confronting it without comforting erasures. The controversial Soviet writer and critic Ilya Ehrenburg, a contemporary of the Formalists and of Tatlin, presented a discursive monument to this shared daydreaming after seeing Tatlin's model next to "the dilapidated buildings blackened from stoves reeking":

> It was all very moving. Soviet office workers were moving off with their rations of horse meat. A boy was selling cake crumbs; as for me, I was in the middle of a square where in the civilized era there used to be almost a little garden. I stood together with two artists and we dreamed about the possibilities of iron. The cold made us go back and forth in one place and gesticulate as if we were passionate southerners. We were absorbed in the state of daydreaming after seeing the model for the Monument to the Third International by Tatlin, and not without reason. A self-taught white-browed prophet (resembling an artisan) had placed on the ruins of the imperial Petersburg a clear sign: the beginning of a new architecture.
>
> Let us briefly recall his merits. In the midst of an epidemic of plaster idiots (*gipsovye kretiny*) quartered on our squares by the cunning of a superior power (thank God for rain and wind —only for a short time!) came suddenly something simple and clear; enough my bearded friends, stop playing with dolls.[35]

Among those "plaster idiots" of the postrevolutionary "monumental propaganda" that was announced by Lenin and attacked by Ehrenburg was Karl Marx himself, whose plaster head had been trimmed by an Assyrian barber, as a tribute to contemporary thought.[36] Tatlin's project defied the budding cults of the Leader and the Party. It estranged both the difficult circumstances of the present and an emergent Soviet architecture of the future that returned to traditional forms and became dependent upon Stalin's personal approval. Ehrenburg offers a slice of life of the postrevolutionary era that gives us insight into the narrative life of architecture as a laboratory of consciousness.

But the most striking assessment of Tatlin's monument would come from Sergei Eisenstein himself, the son of a prominent Riga architect, who tried to redefine architectural space in his films and in his theoretical essays—far beyond his father's modernist eclecticism. In the early 1930s, at the time of the official declaration of Socialist Realism, Eisenstein, like many of his fellow avant-gardists, was experiencing difficulties with the production and reception of his films, and therefore returned to writing and to his theory of montage. In his essay "Pathos" he advanced the interesting concept of the "architecture of suspension." If Tatlin and Malevich saw in the tower a synthesis between architecture and sculpture, Eisenstein added other dimensions of literature and cinema, going back to a forgotten essay on architecture written by Nikolai Gogol in 1831:

> "So far the architecture of suspension has manifested itself only in theater boxes, balconies, and small bridges [wrote Gogol]. But what if ... these transparent cast-iron decorations wrapped around a wondrous beautiful tower, and rose with it to the sky ..." Andrey Bely once astonished his readers with a quotation from Gogol's "Nevsky Prospect" that anticipated Picasso. But Bely overlooked for some reason the fact that Gogol also anticipated Le Corbusier's ideas of a house on columns; and if his idea of architecture's transparency is not solved by a transparent veil of cast-iron, then it is solved with glass, as proposed by the American Frank Lloyd Wright, and with the idea of the "wondrous tower"—which is Tatlin's Tower.... "What a wealth of suggestions [Gogol concludes] have been put forward, which can give birth to a completely new idea in the head of an architect, provided this architect is—a creator and a poet."[37]

In Borgesian fashion, Eisenstein advances the paradoxical argument that Gogol's literary musings at once prefigured and are illuminated by Tatlin's Tower. Eisenstein made a theoretical montage of imaginary and real architecture, creating his own genealogy of styles and working against the irreversibility of time. Estrangement offers not only reverse mimesis but a liberating side-move, which allowed a frustrated filmmaker to become a visionary theorist and explore the conjectural histories of different media.

Around the same time as Eisenstein described the "architecture of suspension," Walter Benjamin developed his own conception of allegorical architecture. For Benjamin, an allegorical architecture had the capacity to put new technological materials such as iron to artistic use. A castiron Saturn on the balcony of a Parisian bourgeois apartment, *à la* Grandville, became the very figure of allegory for modern melancholia. In Benjamin's view, the new architectural use of iron and glass signified not merely technological "progress," but rather a particular dialectical tension between art and technology, artifice and nature. Technology ennobled itself by appealing to the prestige of the arts, and the arts followed by expropriating the new technology for their own use. In his Arcades Project, Benjamin offered the concept of the "dialectic at a standstill," viewing the nineteenth-century passage-building as halfway between art and utility and between utopia and commercialism: "For the first time in the history of architecture, an artificial building material appears: iron…. Iron is avoided in home construction but used in arcades, exhibition halls, train stations—buildings that serve transitory purposes."[38]

If we compare the architecture of the arcades (as described by Benjamin) and of Tatlin's Tower, and substitute state utilitarianism for commercial utilitarianism, we discover a similarly oxymoronic dialectic that crystallizes the paradoxes of the specific historical moment. It is curious that during his fateful journey to Moscow in the winter of 1926–27, Benjamin made very few comments about the new architecture. In fact, instead of commenting on the new projects, he visited such untouristic and outmoded places as the outdoor market, the toy museum, the ruined towers of old Moscow—a choice of sites that uncannily became prophetic. Benjamin described the exact sites that would be slated for demolition owing to their supposed counterrevolutionary "backwardness" just a few years after Benjamin's trip. This was during the realization of Stalin's plan of transforming Moscow into an ideal communist city, a radical twentieth-century version of "Hausmannization." Benjamin's materialist method led him to intuit this imminent historical change and to experience an acute anticipatory nostalgia that turned out to predict the future accurately. His profound insight in this case was a result of the particular method that he pursued in his research—a method that was not mystical but rather material and imaginative. It was predicated on a risky double movement between theory and experience, between the art of looking and the art of thinking. In Moscow, he observed, one had to question all preconceptions, both that of the Western "bourgeois" discourses and that of the starry-eyed Marxism of the party line. Benjamin refused to offer any "theory" about the Soviet experience, claiming enigmatically in a letter to Martin Buber that in Moscow "all factuality is already theory." The role of the critic, then, was to collect those slices of life and "facts" of the fleeting present in the land of the future.[39] "Fact" does not refer here to a positivistic notion of facticity, but rather to the Constructivist concept of *faktura*, close to German "new objectivity." While capturing the materiality of daily existence, such "facts" in the writings of both Shklovsky and Benjamin always hover on the brink of allegory; sometimes, the closer they get to a direct description of material experience, the more "auratic" and aphoristic they become. Thus Benjamin too practiced a particular third way of thinking, between description of urban experience and a critical theory that defamiliarized both. While not finding much avant-garde architecture in Moscow, Benjamin developed an off-modern way of seeing the postrevolutionary city in which "the modern ... is always citing primal history."[40]

    The eccentric survival of Tatlin's Tower in oral histories went hand in hand with the forgetting of Tatlin the artist.

The Berlin Dada artist George Grosz, who met Tatlin in the 1920s, visited him once again right before his death. "I went to see Tatlin once more. He lived in a small, old, dilapidated apartment.... There was a completely rusted wire mattress leaning on the wall behind him with a few sleeping chickens sitting on it, their heads tucked under their wings. They furnished the perfect frame to dear Tatlin as he started to play his homemade balalaika.... We suddenly seemed surrounded by the melancholy humor of a book by Gogol. Tatlin was no longer the ultramodern constructivist; he was a piece of genuine, old Russia."[41] Like many well-wishing Western artists visiting Stalin's Russia, Grosz did not realize that the decrepit conditions and poverty of Tatlin's apartment and his isolated lifestyle were not due to some exotic Russian eccentricity but to the specific circumstances of experimental art in the Soviet Union. Tatlin was fortunate to die a natural death —coincidentally the same year as Stalin and Dziga Vertov.

Installation-Architecture and Contemporary Ruinophilia

In 1998 the Russian-American architect and designer Constantin Boym made a series of souvenirs of missing monuments. There was a little bronze souvenir of Tatlin's Tower along with ones of the Palace of the Soviets and the Temple of King Solomon. Tatlin's revolutionary Tower of Babel found its second life as an artistic myth; it became a phantom limb of the nonconformist tradition of twentieth-century art, cropping up in paper architecture, conceptual installations, and urban folklore.

Many of the artists known as Moscow Conceptualists, a loosely organized movement that included Ilya Kabakov, Vitaly Komar and Alexander Melamid, Alexander Kosolepov, Igor Makarevich and Elena Elagina, and Leonid Sokov, recycled Tatlin's Tower and other inspirational icons of the avant-garde, together with Soviet everyday trash and the symbols of official ideological art. They performed a transcultural hyperexchange, translating political objects of the Soviet era into artistic signs. If Western artists were often fascinated by the visionary potential and bold exoticism of the Soviet utopia, Soviet artists now confronted this utopia's metamorphosis in their daily practices of art and life. More deeply connected to their status as ruins, they proved to be less reverential toward them. They approached avant-garde objects without museum pieties. In fact, in their memory, the international avant-garde was never part of a museum culture or art market; it had no official museal sacrality. Instead, it belonged to the reservoir of unofficial utopian dreams.

Tatlin's Tower played a prominent role in the invisible cities of this alternative cultural imagination. It became a central monument in the paper architecture and installation art of the 1970s through the 1990s. Paper architecture emerged in 1970 as a way of recycling and remembering the utopian dreams of the 1920s. It did not try to make fairytales come true; quite the contrary. The paper architects—young architects who had studied in the Moscow Architectural Institute, the successor of the famous VKhUTEMAS of the 1920s—were proud to work with paper, not stone and concrete. They led a parallel existence in which they dedicated themselves to international architectural competitions, winning many of them. These young and brilliant architects regarded project-making, rather than building, as a way of life. They inhabited their mythical worlds lightly, as extraterritorials traveling beyond the Iron Curtain through the vehicle of their designs even when they themselves could not. Immateriality was almost a sign of integrity; these architects did not want to compromise the radicality of their imagination, and they took the life of their projects more seriously than their job in the Soviet architectural industry (if they had one). While the Western followers of the Russian avant-garde embraced the original social message of the movement and tried to be as utopian as possible, the Russian architects embraced the artistic potential, blatantly defying official collective imperatives. Thus, if the artists from the two sides of the Iron Curtain shared forms, they did not share their cultural signification or affective memory.

Although Tatlin's Tower shows up in the work of many

of these Russian artists and architects, they each create a different afterlife, or half-life, for it. In the studio of Leonid Sokov, one of the Conceptualist artists who can actually make you laugh, models and limbs of Tatlin's Tower in different scales lie around like discarded children's toys, souvenirs or amateur architectural projects. The tower is young again, one can play with it, rediscover its sculptural, political, and ludic potentials. Sokov's is definitely a tactile conceptualism, encouraging you to play with every vertebra of cultural memory and experimental art.

In one of Sokov's works, Madonna and Child, Tatlin's Tower appears as a holy ghost, a Madonna-shaped, Magritte-style cutout that encloses a desolate Russian landscape. Here the tower is placed into a natural setting and framed as an unconventional icon of nonconformist art. In Sokov's work the famous ruin of the avant-garde acquires a fragile anthropomorphic physicality. It is no longer made of the thin air of revolution but of rough wood that leaves splinters under your skin and is modern and primitive at once.

In a dialogue about Sokov's work, cultural theorist Viktor Tupitsyn and Ilya Kabakov raise an important question: "Is he a post-modernist or a folklorist?"[42] Sokov's ludic sculptures reveal the corporeality of the utopian ideology, its carnivalesque body. Yet this is not a stylized Bakhtinian-Rabelaisian carnivalesque, but impure and hybrid Soviet everyday art. It foregrounds marginal and secondary layers of non-artistic culture that, according to Shklovsky and Tynianov's conceptions of filiation and literary evolution, offer new possibilities for an artistic innovation that does not always look backward or forward but often sideways, following the movements of the chess knight. In the case of Sokov this secondary cultural field includes military culture, Soviet graffiti art (*zabornaia kul'tura*), official propaganda, and everyday anti-design.

Sokov's rough, unfinished sculptures have another, less mythical source of inspiration. While enrolled as an art student in the university, Sokov served in the Soviet army. Looking through the military library, he discovered by chance the 1930s account of an artists' and writers' journey to the Belomor Canal construction site. Even though this was official Soviet propaganda, it had a striking appeal. Sokov was struck by the photographs of the Gulag instruments of slave labor, which revealed the brutal and premodern manner in which Soviet industrial might came into being. In his spare time, he filled his sketchbooks with drawings of these primitive modern machines and the frightening architecture of the labor camps. In his later work he stages the uncanny metamorphosis of a tower—the Tower of Babel, Tatlin's Tower, the Ur-Neo-Geo-Tower of the Neo-Avant-Garde—and a hyperrealistic watchtower of the Gulag. Sokov also made a life-size sculptural portrait of the contemporary artist as a Gulag guard next to the wooden watchtower. This is a revealing cultural self-fashioning: the artist does not present himself as a glamorous nonconformist next to the liberating spiral tower, but as a cog in the system guarding a model watchtower that resembles the memorial to the avant-garde dream. The relationship between Tatlin's Tower and the watchtower of the Gulag is not to be taken literally. Tatlin's Tower did not "lead" to the watchtower of the Gulag. They are not part of the same "total work of Stalinism"; they do not suggest a direct continuity between avant-garde utopianism and the official teleology of the Stalinist state. In contrast to Groys's Total Art of Stalinism (although extremely provocative and timely when it was conceived in the late 1980s as an antidote both to Soviet and Russian forgetting of socialist realism and to Western heroization of the avant-garde), a twenty-first-century perspectival "ruin-gaze" demands a more nuanced approach that maps artistic and state zones with precision. The avant-garde was a diverse phenomenon and no blanket statement of analogy between artistic and social revolution adequately describes its historical specificity. Tatlin's unfinished tower did not "evolve" into a roughly constructed yet efficient watchtower of the Gulag. Rather, they both belonged to the same cultural landscape of Soviet modernity: the ruins of one point to the invisible ruins of the other.

Even nonconformist artists rarely spoke directly about the

Gulag in spite of the fact that camp survivors lived among them and the Gulag experience was still a living memory. The reasons for this are complex. Direct political speech of any kind was seen as "aesthetically incorrect," too ideological even if aimed against the official ideology. Nonconformist artists developed their alternative subculture after the Thaw and reacted against the "sincere" and direct lyricism of 1960s art and writing. It is possible that they also internalized Soviet cultural taboos and worked with silences, hinting at cultural traumas but not disclosing them explicitly. The Gulag was not a death camp even though the amount of senseless cruelty, death, and murder that took place there rivals the Nazi camps. It was a slave labor camp, a living camp, and a part of the Soviet territory that overlapped with the rest of the country in many invisible ways. Rediscovering these haunting presences in this artistic work is like developing the invisible layers of the film of memory. Conceptual installations and sculptures have reproduced the territories of terror of Soviet life, trying but not always succeeding in estranging it.

Sokov is one of the few artists whose works comment on the artistic complicity with the official *ars oblivionalis* and engage with the surviving ruins of the "zone." The seemingly neutral and foreign word "zone" had a special meaning in Soviet Russia. It was a bureaucratic euphemism for prison and the Gulag. The word became so influential in the culture that the world outside the "zone" was not called the "free world" but the "free zone." Sokov places avant-garde monuments into a new cultural context that is not merely postmodern but border-zone, the space of unofficial and informal architecture of fences and locks, of nondescript maintenance buildings, no-man's-lands that bear a patina of repressed history. His materials are those of the zone that he tried to transport into the "free zone" of his imagination. In Sokov's work postmodernity quotes prehistory. Or perhaps, as Kabakov suggests, postmodernity in his work becomes a living memory: losing its cerebral quotation marks, it turns into an occasion for physical comedy or boundless melancholy. Tatlin's Tower, a virtual ruin, acquires materiality. Its dysfunctionality and virtuality make it not less but more important and credible for the theater of cultural memory. For the artists of the 1970s, Letatlin's bones and the Tower's architectural carcass are no longer mere symbols or models; they acquire a fragmentary body and become part of the ludic cultural archaeology of the twentieth century. To quote Kabakov, "The naive world of Sokov is not so naive."[43]

Others have used the tower not as material but as a kind of dwelling. Architect Yuri Avvakumov created the <u>Perestroika Tower</u> (1990), incorporating Boris Iofan and Vera Mukhina's sculpture <u>Worker and Collective Farmer</u> (1936–37), one of Socialist Realism's masterpieces. As if following Trotsky's description of Tatlin's Tower as a giant scaffolding, Avvakumov makes a monument out of construction cranes that resemble children's toys.[44] Unlike Sokov's discarded toys, however, these create an environment, a harbor for both art and people. Avvakumov's relationship to the tower is affectionate and tender as well as ironic. Tatlin's model turns into a shelter for unlikely tenants—not only the ideal peasant and worker, but also all the dreamers of the future.

Artistic installations are another form of nonfunctional architecture that provide a refuge for the real and virtual ruins of the avant-garde. In a more recent work, <u>The Palace of Projects</u> (1995–2001), Kabakov, one of the pioneers of the "total installation," encompassing ruins, souvenirs, models, and everyday trash, finds a new function for Tatlin's Tower.[45] <u>The Palace of Projects</u> becomes the artist's exilic habitat, housing many mini-utopias. The Tower's spiral shape determines the ambivalent form of the installation: it evokes the shape of both archetypal modern museums like the Guggenheim in New York and, at the same time, a snail's shell, which appears in many of Kabakov's drawings. The gravity-defying avant-garde monument is now transformed into the protective shell of the snail's transient artistic domesticity, becoming the portable home of immigrant dreams.

<u>The Palace of Projects</u> exemplifies Kabakov's work of memory. A complete environment, it incorporates the artist's earlier works, fragments from his albums, paintings, everyday objects, collectibles from obsessive communal apartment

neighbors, unfinished masterpieces of the avant-garde, sketches by untalented artists, and communal trash. Moreover, as the artist observed about one of the showings of the project, visitors began to leave their personal belongings, as if the installation had turned into an international storage space for nostalgic refuse. In another way, it helped people to transform their useless objects into works of art. Kabakov thus promoted a tactile conceptualism, a game of hide-and-seek with aesthetic distance itself. In the end, <u>The Palace of Projects</u> was a unique museum of dreams, hypotheses, and projects predicated on the shared belief that to "lead a worthy human life is to have one's own project."[46]

In Kabakov's view, everyone should be given an equal right to exhibit the models of his or her desire. Instead of building one group's utopia on a real scale, the artist proposes to give people a chance to show their dream worlds—in miniature. If only Hitler had presented a miniature version of the Third Reich to the applause of the Viennese artistic establishment, twentieth-century history might have been different!

There were many cosmic dreams in Kabokov's palace, miniature Letatlins born in the claustrophobic conditions of crowded communal living. Each project had a small room of its own, although there were also empty rooms for the reluctant dreamers of the future and for projects that were submitted belatedly and missed all possible deadlines. There, the visitor could sit in solitude on a chair and inhabit someone else's fantasy, "co-experience it," and become inspired. Almost every project had an author: an ordinary dreamer, a provincial eccentric, an amateur scientist, a self-made philosopher of the universe, an untalented artist, or an unrecognized genius. In this project undertaken in exile, the artist's strategy became bicultural, combining the Western language of therapy and home-improvement with the Eastern fantasies of flight and escape, practical American dreams with Russian aspirations to change the world. <u>The Palace of Projects</u> was a grandiose hybrid of cross-cultural dreams and obsessions, a cross between a utopian projection and a ten-step program for self-improvement.

For Kabakov, the total installation thus becomes a home away from home. It helps him to dislocate and estrange the topography of his childhood fears, and to domesticate it again abroad. To borrow Jean-François Lyotard's category, "domestication without domus" is a way of inhabiting one's displaced habitats and avoiding the extremes of both the *domus* of traditional family values and the megapolis of global or cyberspace.[47] Ultimately, what Kabokov's projects "install" is not space but time. If past and future are embodied in his installations in the shapes and location of objects, the present is personified by the visitor herself. The "spirals of time," in Kabakov's description, pierce through her and unwind in different directions.

Kabakov's work is also about the selectiveness of memory. His fragmented "total installations" become a cautious reminder of gaps, compromises, embarrassments, and black holes in the foundations of any utopian edifice. Ambiguous longing for the past is linked to the individual experience of history. Combining empathy with estrangement, his ironic nostalgia invites viewers to reflect on the ethics of remembering. Further, Kabakov goes to the origins of modern utopia and reveals two contradictory human impulses: to transcend the everyday in some kind of collective fairytale, and to inhabit the most uninhabitable ruins, to survive while preserving memories. His installation art exhibits the failure of the teleology of progress. Instead of some singular, unifying, and dazzling Palace of the Future, what is on display are the scattered models of past and future. Kabakov's total installations reveal a nostalgia for utopia, but they return utopia to its origins—not in life, but in art.

In his recent projects, Kabakov has also tended to choose industrial ruins and remainders of large projects of modernization for his installations. The Palace of Projects was installed at the Armory in New York and at the Kokerei Zollverein in Essen, Germany. His installations amid the industrial ruins highlight a trend in contemporary art and architecture that follows the best traditions of the off-modern in the rethinking of *techne*, estrangement, and toleration for the ruins of modernity.

From the Tate Modern in London to Mass MoCA in North Adams, Massachusetts, and in various artistic projects from those of Gordon Matta-Clark to those of Jane and Louise Wilson, we can observe this fascinating intersection between architecture, installation art and experimental literature. Tatlin's Tower haunts these conceptual works like a specter of lost opportunities. In Robert Smithson's "Entropic Landscapes," "Spirals," and "Spiral Jetties," Tatlin meets Jorge Luis Borges and Vladimir Nabokov in the parallel universe of the American landscape. Here Tatlin's ruins/construction sites, Borgesian "circular ruins," and the spirals of Nabokov's imagination compose an eccentric museum of the alternative architecture of the twentieth century.[48] The Wilsons' Free and Anonymous Monument, a project based on decaying postwar modern architecture, produces flickering shapes of Tatlin's Tower using cinematic projection.[49] Similarly, in some of Matta-Clark's "cuts" through buildings slated for demolition, Tatlin's Tower, the model of a future architecture, appears *via negativa*—in the shapes of the cut itself, which echoes its Babelian spiral.

In these architectural and artistic projects that recycle industrial forms and materials, the off-modern reveals itself in the form of a paradoxical ruinophilia. New buildings or installations neither destroy the past nor rebuild it; rather, the architect or the artist co-creates with remainders of history, collaborates with modern ruins, redefines their functions— both utilitarian and poetic. The resulting eclectic transitional architecture promotes a spatial and temporal extension into the past and the future, into different existential topographies of cultural forms. The off-modern gaze acknowledges the disharmony and the ambivalent relationship between human, historical, and natural temporalities. It reconciles itself to perspectivism and conjectural history. Thus the off-modern perspective allows us to frame utopian projects as dialectical ruins—not to discard or demolish them, but rather to confront and incorporate them into our own fleeting present.

In her last book, The Life of the Mind, Hannah Arendt proposed a distinction between "professional thinking," which focuses on disciplinarity and logical coherence, and "passionate thinking," which explores the limits of knowledge and is guided by wonder, not by the need for systematicity and consistency. Off-modern thinking is a form of passionate thinking engaged in a double movement between theory and practice, between imaginary architecture and material experience.[50]

Notes

1. Georges Bataille, "Slaughterhouse," in Encyclopaedia Acephalica (London: Atlas Press, 1995), 73.
2. For a different way of thinking about architecture, see Kenneth Frampton, "The Status of Man and the Status of His Objects: A Reading of The Human Condition," in Labor, Work, and Architecture (London: Phaidon, 2002), 24–43.
3. Georg Simmel, "The Adventurer," in On Individuality and Social Forms, ed. Donald Levine (Chicago: University of Chicago Press, 1971), 187–198. Simmel's theory of adventure was in itself a disciplinary adventure, a critique of the capitalist commodification of daily life but also an alternative to the disparaging Marxist conception of the public realm and civil society, and to Weber's and Lukacs's understanding of modernity as disenchantment and transcendental homelessness. Simmel himself fit neither into the German academic establishment of his time nor into contemporary disciplinary systems of thought. Adventure was not only his topic but also an intellectual and existential *modus operandi*.
4. Simmel, "The Adventurer," 189–94.
5. Ibid.
6. I refer here to Rosalind Krauss, The Originality of the Avant-Garde and Other Modernist Myths (Cambridge, MA: MIT Press, 1985), and to Boris Groys, The Total Art of Stalinism: Avant-Garde, Aesthetic Dictatorship, and Beyond, trans. Charles Rougle (Princeton: Princeton University Press, 1992), whose ideas have shaped contradictory attitudes toward the avant-garde.
7. Leon Trotsky, Literatur und Revolution (Vienna: Verlag für Literatur und Politik, 1924). In English, see Literature and Revolution, trans. Rose Strunsky (Ann Arbor, MI: University of Michigan Press, 1971), 246–47. Unattributed translations from the Russian here and elsewhere are by the author.
8. Nikolai Punin, Pamiatnik tret'emu internatsionalu (Petrograd: Otdel IZO Narkomprossa, 1921), 2.
9. El Lissitzky, "Basic Premises, Interrelationships between the Arts, the New City, and Ideological Superstructure," in Bolshevik Visions, vol. 2, ed. William G. Rosenberg (Ann Arbor: University of Michigan, 1990), 188.
10. For more information on the iconography of the tower, see John Elderfield, "The Line of Free Men: Tatlin's 'Towers' and the Age of Invention," Studio International, vol. 178, no. 916 (Nov 1969), 165. Elderfield notes that the ziggurat at Babylon is "the house of the foundation of heaven and earth, and its symbolism that of the holy mountain, and the spiral stair the path to its summit." Elderfield also compares the form of the spiral to the "figura serpentina" in Mannerist and Baroque architecture, and discusses Sigfried Giedion's comparison of Tatlin's Tower to the spiral lantern of Borromini's St. Ivo della Sapienza. In the present essay, I am interested not in symbolic forms of consciousness, but in the existence of forms in the world and in human creativity.
11. Roland Barthes, "The Eiffel Tower," in The Eiffel Tower, and Other Mythologies, trans. Richard Howard (New York: Noonday Press/Farrar, Straus & Giroux, 1979), 3–18.
12. See Anatoly Strigalev and Jürgen Harten, Vladimir Tatlin, Retrospektive (Cologne: DuMont Buchverlag, 1993), 37.
13. Lissitzky, "Basic Premises," 188.
14. Two centuries ago, Friedrich Schlegel commented on the pace of transformation of modern ruins: "Many of the works of the Ancients have become fragments. Many of the works of the Moderns are fragments the moment they come into being." Quoted in Irresistible Decay: Ruins Reclaimed, ed. Michael S. Roth with Claire Lyons and Charles Merewether (Los Angeles: Getty Research Institute for the History of Art and the Humanities, 1997), 72.
15. See Svetlana Boym, "Kosmos: Remembrances of the Future," in Adam Bartos, Kosmos: A Portrait of the Russian Space Age (New York: Princeton Architectural Press, 2001), 80–99.
16. Strigalev and Harten, Vladimir Tatlin, Retrospektive, 394.
17. Contemporary artist Leonid Sokov recalls that in the 1970s, various elderly women who worked in the mosaic factory where Tatlin was employed during the last years of his life or in the local theaters brought with them small pictures of Tatlin's forgotten still lifes, which the artist apparently gave them in exchange for money and food.
18. See Svetlana Boym, The Future of Nostalgia (New York: Basic Books, 2001), 100–108.
19. Viktor Shklovsky, "Pamiatnik tret'emu internatsionalu," in Khod konia: sbornik statei (Moscow and Berlin: Gelikon: 1923), 108–111. In English see "The Monument to the Third International," in The Knight's Move, trans. Richard Sheldon (Dalkey Archive Press, 2005), 69–70.
20. Shklovsky, The Knight's Move, trans. Richard Sheldon, 70. Translation slightly modified.
21. Ibid.
22. The statue was erected by the sculptor Paolo Trubetskoi in 1909 on Znamensky Square near the Nicholas Station, now Vosstania Square near the Moscow Railway Station.
23. Viktor Shklovsky, "Svobodnyi port" in Khod konia: sbornik statei, 196–97. In English see "A Free Port" in The Knight's Move, trans. Richard Sheldon, 126–27.

24. This "oblique" ludic architecture may be compared to the Baroque figure of anamorphosis. As in Holbein's famous painting The Ambassadors (1533), it reveals the skulls and "skeletons" in the closet of the revolution, which are represented here by the dangerous games of street kids trying to escape from revolutionary reeducation. I am grateful to Tatiana Smoliarova for drawing my attention to the concept of anamorphosis.

25. Victor Shklovsky, "Art as Technique," in Russian Formalist Criticism: Four Essays, ed. and trans. Lee T. Lemon and Marion J. Reis (Lincoln: University of Nebraska Press, 1965), 3–24. In Russian, "Iskusstvo kak priem," O teorii prozy (Moscow: Sovetskii pisatel, 1983). For a detailed discussion, see Svetlana Boym, "Poetics and Politics of Estrangement: Victor Shklovsky and Hannah Arendt," Poetics Today, vol. 26, no. 4 (2005), 581–611.

26. In his first revolutionary exercise in literary criticism, "The Resurrection of the Word" (1914), which he read on the stage of the Stray Dog Cabaret, Shklovsky describes the ornamental and nonfunctional arches of the nearby historicist eclectic building on Nevsky Avenue as examples of "architectural absurdity" and a habitual disregard for structures and functions. Viktor Shklovsky, Gamburgskii schet: stat'i—vospominaniia—esse (1914–1933) (Moscow: Sovetskii pisatel, 1990), unpag. Throughout the 1920s Shklovsky developed his own conception of parallelism. The word "parallel" here may be misleading, especially from the conventional Euclidean perspective. To borrow Nabokov's description of the Gogolian version of Lobachevsky's geometry: "If the parallel lines do not meet, it is not because meet they cannot, but because they have other things to do." Vladimir Nabokov, Lectures on Russian Literature, ed. Fredson Bowers (New York: Harcourt Brace Jovanovich/Bruccoli Clark, 1981), 58. Shklovsky's literary parallelisms hesitate between irony, analogy, and allegory, all rhetorical figures based on doubleness, double entendre, or speaking otherwise.

27. Shklovsky, "Vstuplenie pervoe" in Khod konia: sbornik statei, 9–10. In English see "First Preface," in The Knight's Move, trans. Richard Sheldon, 3–4.

28. Lydia Ginsburg, "Zapiski" (1927) in Chelovek za pis'mennym stolom (Leningrad: Sovetskii pisatel, 1989), 59.

29. Viktor Shklovsky, Tret'ia fabrika (Moscow: Krug: 1926), 47–49. For background in English, see Richard Sheldon, "Viktor Shklovsky and the Device of Ostensible Surrender," in Viktor Shklovsky, Third Factory, ed. and trans. Richard Sheldon (Ann Arbor, MI: Ardis, 1977), vii–xxx.

30. Hannah Arendt, "What Is Freedom?" in Between Past and Future (London: Penguin, 1979), 143–73.

31. Arendt, "What Is Freedom?" 143.

32. Within the Formalist tradition one can distinguish between the theorists who moved toward structuralist linguistics and developed a binary structure of thinking, and those who oriented themselves toward cultural theory. The best-known representative of the former group is Roman Jakobson, who was largely responsible for the early interpretations of Formalist theory and history. However, theorists and critics less well-known in the West, including Shklovsky, Yuri Tynianov, Boris Eikhenbaum, and Boris Tomashevsky, gravitated toward a third way of thinking, especially in the realm of culture.

33. Kazimir Malevich, "On Tatlin," in Novaia Generatsiia (Kharkov) 8 (1929); trans. in Troels Andersen, Vladimir Tatlin, Moderna museets katalog, vol.75 (Stockholm: Moderna Museet, 1968), 66.

34. Stephen Bann, introduction, in Global Conceptualism: Points of Origin, 1950–1980, exhibition catalogue (New York: Queens Museum of Art, New York, 1999), 73–84.

35. Ilya Ehrenburg, E pur se muove (Berlin: Gelicon, 1922), 18.

36. Ehrenburg, E pur se muove, 18–22.

37. Sergei Eisenstein, "Pathos" (1946), in Izbrannye proizvedeniia, vol. 3 (Moscow: 1964), 198. In English see "Pathos" in Nonindifferent nature, trans. Herbert Marshall (Cambridge, MA: Cambridge University Press, 1987), 165.

38. Walter Benjamin, "Paris, the Capital of the Nineteenth Century," in The Arcades Project, trans. Howard Eiland and Kevin McLaughlin (Cambridge, MA: Belknap Press, 1999), 4.

39. Walter Benjamin, Moscow Diary, ed. Gary Smith, trans. Richard Sieburth (Cambridge, MA: Harvard University Press, 1986), 132.

40. Walter Benjamin, "Paris, the Capital of the Nineteenth Century," 10.

41. George Grosz, An Autobiography, trans. Nora Hodges of Ein kleines Ja und ein grosses Nein (New York: Macmillan, 1983), 179–80.

42. "A Conversation between Victor Tupitsyn and Ilya Kabakov on Leonid Sokov" in Leonid Sokov: Sculptures, Paintings, Objects, Installations, Documents, Articles (St. Petersburg: State Russian Museum, The Palace Edition, 2000), 15–16.

43. "A Conversation between Victor Tupitsyn and Ilya Kabakov on Leonid Sokov," 16.

44. For a more detailed discussion, see Constantin Boym, New Russian Design (New York: Rizzoli International Publications, 1992).

45. Kabakov turned to the total installation in the late 1980s, but after his departure from the Soviet

Union in 1990 and the end of the Soviet Union in 1991, the total installation became the artist's dominant genre. Currently Kabakov lives in voluntary exile in the United States. For a detailed discussion of Kabakov's conception of installation and the uses of nostalgia, see Svetlana Boym, The Future of Nostalgia, 309–327, and Boris Groys, The Total Art of Stalinism, 84–89.
46. Svetlana Boym, interview with Ilya Kabakov, May 1999.
47. Jean-François Lyotard, "Domus and Megapolis," in The Inhuman: Reflections on Time, trans. Geoffrey Bennington and Rachel Bowlby (Stanford, CA: Stanford University Press, 1991). Andreas Huyssen, in his book Twilight Memories: Marking Time in a Culture of Amnesia (New York: Routledge, 1995), 35, claims that the current memory boom is not a result of further kitschification of the past, but "a potentially healthy sign of contestation; a contestation of the informational hyperspace and an expression of the basic human need to live in extended structures of temporality, however they may be organized.... In that dystopian vision of the high-tech future, amnesia would no longer be part of the dialectics of memory and forgetting. It will be its radical other. It will have sealed the very forgetting of memory itself: nothing to remember, nothing to forget."
48. For a discussion of Smithson's favorite literary texts, see Thomas Crow, "Cosmic Exile: Prophetic Turns in the Life and Art of Robert Smithson," 32–80, and Richard Sieburth, "A Heap of Language: Robert Smithson and American Hieroglyphics," 218–24, both in Robert Smithson (Los Angeles: Museum of Contemporary Art, 2004).
49. For a detailed discussion of this project, see Giuliana Bruno, "Modernist Ruins, Filmic Archaeologies: Jane and Louise Wilson's A Free and Anonymous Monument" (2004), in Public Intimacy: Architecture and the Visual Arts (Cambridge MA: MIT Press, 2007).
50. Hannah Arendt, The Life of the Mind (New York: Harcourt Brace Jovanovich, 1978), 2, 5–7, 198–99.
51. Walter Benjamin, "Short Shadows," trans. Rodney Livingstone, in Selected Writings, vol. 2, pt. 1 (Cambridge, MA: Harvard University Press, 2004), 701.

1 Still from the film <u>Tatlin's Tower</u>, 1999, produced and directed by Takehiko Nagakura.
Color altered by Svetlana Boym with permission of the filmmaker

2 Construction of the model of Tatlin's Tower, 1920. Bottom from left to right: Sofia Dymshits-Tolstaya, Vladimir Tatlin, T. Shapiro, and I. Meyerzon

3 The Tatlin Studio Collective in front of the model of Tatlin's Tower, in the Mosaics Studio of the former Academy of Arts, Petrograd, November 1920. Tatlin third from left

4 The Tower of Babel, from Athanasius Kircher's Turris Babel, 1679

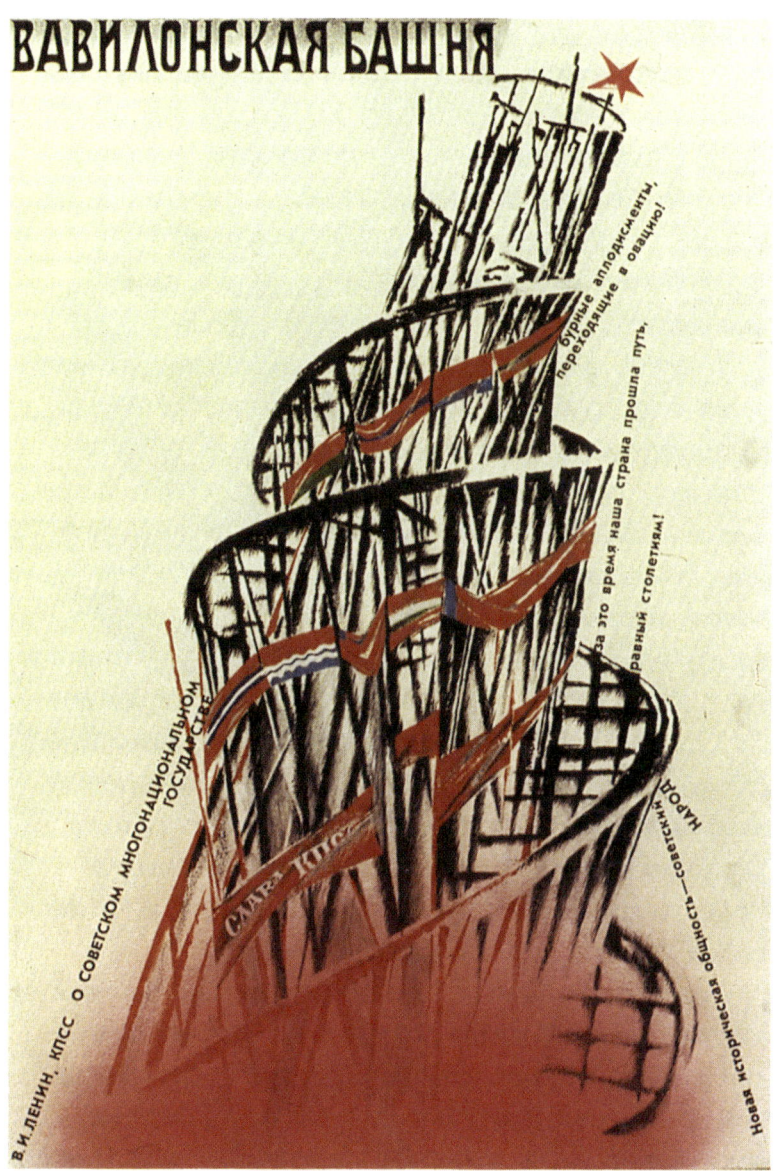

5 Natalia Verdi, Babylonian Tower, poster, from Moscou s'affiche, 1991

6 A simplified model of Tatlin's Tower at the May Day parade, Leningrad, 1926

7 The artists George Grosz and John Heartfield with a placard inscribed "Art is dead: Long live the machine art of Tatlin," First International Dada Fair, Berlin, 1920

8 The second model of Tatlin's Tower at the International Exhibition of Decorative and Industrial Arts, Paris, 1925. Photograph: Alexander Rodchenko

9 Flight tests with Letatlin, summer 1932

10 Letatlin exhibited in the Museum of State Art, Moscow, 1932

11 Fuselage of Letatlin, 1932

12 Vladimir Mayakovsky's catafalque in his funeral procession in Moscow, April 19, 1930. The catafalque was constructed of iron plates by Tatlin and his students at the VKhUTEIN.

13 Alexander Rodchenko, <u>Last Hour on the Lock</u>, 1934. A staged orchestra of convicts plays a tune for other convicts/ finishing work on a lock.

14 Work on the Belomor canal, 1930–33. Photographer unknown

15 Vladimir Tatlin, White Jar and Potato, 1948–51

16 Vladimir Tatlin, A Skull on an Open Book, 1948–53

17 Vladimir Tatlin, color sketch for the set decoration of Chalice of Joy, 1949–50

18 Vladimir Tatlin, color sketch for the set decoration of Chalice of Joy, 1949–50

19 Boris Iofan, Vladimir Gelfreikh, Vladimir Schuko, and S. Merkulov, Palace of the Soviets, 1946. Rendering of the approved project

20 Model of Tatlin's Tower in the Musée national d'art moderne, Centre Georges Pompidou, Paris, 1979. Photograph: Hervé Lewandowski

21 Model of Tatlin's Tower in the exhibition "Der Traum vom Turm" (The Dream of the Tower) at Forum Kultur und Wirtschaft, Düsseldorf, 2004–5

22 Model of Tatlin's Tower in the Moderna Museet, Stockholm

23 Model of Tatlin's Tower in the New Tretyakov Gallery, Moscow, 1992–93

24 The Soviet "statue of liberty," erected in Vosstania Square, Petrograd (now St. Petersburg), on the first anniversary of the uprising of the Russian Revolution, October 23, 1918

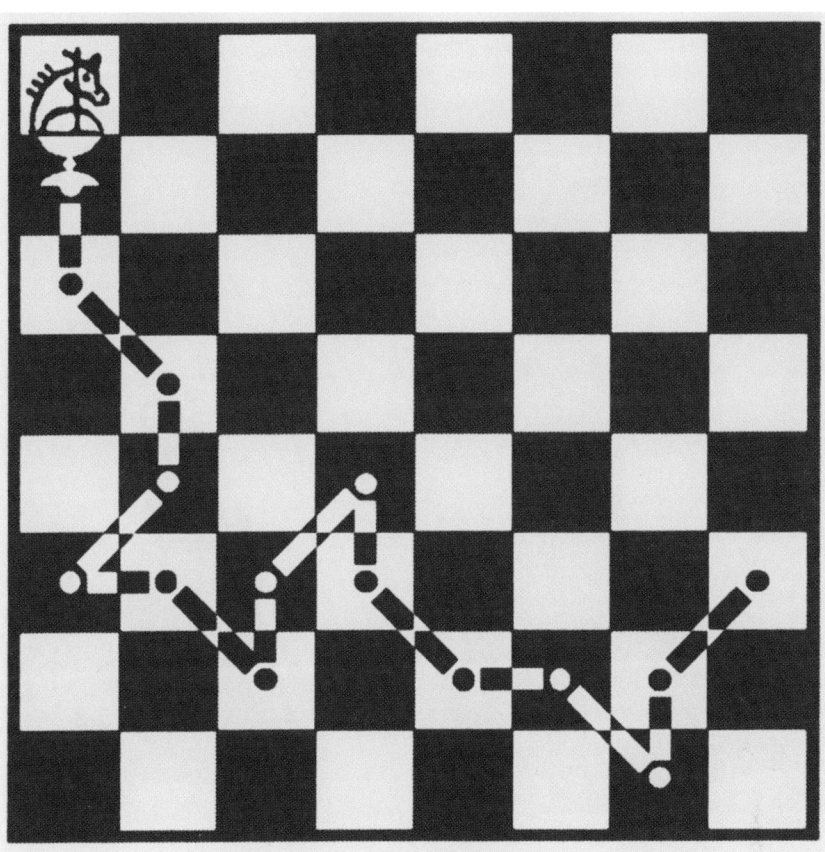

25 Diagram of the knight's move, from Viktor Shklovsky,
Khod konia: sbornik statei, 1923

26 Constantin Boym, Palace of the Soviets and Tatlin's Tower, 1996.
From the series Missing Monuments: Souvenirs for the End of the Century

27 Komar and Melamid, Temple, Exodus from Russia, performance on Mount Zion, Jerusalem, 1978

28 Igor Makarevich and Elena Elagina, Toadstool (with Tatlin's Tower), 2003

29 Leonid Sokov, Mother and Child, 1986

30 Leonid Sokov, Watchtower, Self-Portrait as a Soldier, 1996

31 Ruins of a Gulag tower, 2005. Photograph: Irina Flige

32 Yuri Avvakumov, Perestroika Tower, 1990. This work incorporates Boris Iofan and Vera Mukhina's sculpture Worker and Collective Farmer, 1936–37.

33 Ilya and Emilia Kabakov, The Palace of the Projects, 1995–2001. Installation at the 69th Regiment Armory, New York, 2000. Photograph: Gil Amiaga Foto Studio, Long Island

34 Ilya and Emilia Kabakov, Building of "Contact with the Noosphere," Center for Cosmic Energy, 2000. Photograph: Igoris Markovas

35 Jane and Louise Wilson, Deck, Gorilla VI, A Free and Anonymous Monument, 2003

36 Gordon Matta-Clark, Circus, 1978

37 Robert Smithson, Entropic Landscape, 1970

38 Svetlana Boym, Hybrid Utopias (Tatlin with Butterfly), 2002–7

AN OFF-MODERN MANIFESTO

A Margin of Error

"It's not my fault. Communication error has occurred." My computer pleads with me in a voice called "Victoria." First it excuses itself, then urges me to pay attention, to check my connections, to follow the instructions carefully. I don't. I pull the paper out of the printer prematurely, shattering the image, leaving its outtakes, stripes of transience, inkblots and traces of my hands on the professional glossy surface. Once the disoriented computer spat out a warning across the image "Do Not Copy," an involuntary watermark that emerged from the depth of its disturbed memory. The communication error makes each print unrepeatable and unpredictable. I collect the computer errors. An error has an aura.

To err is human, says a Roman proverb. In advanced technological lingo, the space of humanity itself is relegated to the margin of error. Technology, we are told, is wholly trustworthy, were it not for the human factor. We seem to have gone full circle: to be human means to err. Yet, this margin of error is our margin of freedom. It is a choice beyond the multiple choices programmed for us, an interaction excluded from computerized interactivity. The error is a chance encounter between us and the machines in which we surprise each other. The art of computer erring is neither high tech nor low tech. Rather it's "broken tech." It cheats both on technological progress and on technological obsolescence. And any amateur artist can afford it. Art's new technology is a broken technology.

Or shall we call it dysfunctional, erratic, nostalgic? Nostalgia is a longing for home that no longer exists or most likely, has never existed. That non-existent home is akin to an ideal communal apartment where art and technology co-habited like friendly neighbors or cousins. *Techne*, after all, once referred to arts, crafts, and techniques. Both art and technology were imagined as the forms of human prosthesis, the missing limbs, imaginary or physical extensions of the human space. Many technological inventions, including film and space rockets were first envisioned in science fiction: imagined by artists and writers, not scientists. The term "virtual reality" was in fact coined by Henri Bergson, not Bill Gates. Originally it referred to the virtual realities of human imagination and conscience that couldn't be mimicked by technology. In the early twentieth century the border between art and technology was particularly fertile. Avant-garde artists and critics used the word "technique" to mean an estranging device of art that lays bare the medium and makes us see the world anew. Later, advertisement culture appropriated the avant-garde as one style of many; an exciting marketable look that domesticates, rather than estranges, the utopia of progress. New Hollywood cinema uses most advanced technology to create the special effects. If artistic technique revealed the mechanisms of conscience, the technological special effect domesticates illusions and manipulations.

Has art itself become a mere outtake, a long footnote to the human history? In the United States it is technology, not culture, which is regarded as the space for innovation. Art, it seems, has overstayed its welcome. But amateur artists, immigrants from the disintegrated homeland, survive against all odds. Often they cross the border illegally and, like diasporic repo-men, they try to repossess what used to belong to them, to re-conquer the space of art.

Amateur artists aspire neither for newness nor for a trendy belatedness. The prefixes "avant" and "post" appear equally outdated or irrelevant in the current media age. The same goes for the illusions of "trans." One doesn't have to be "absolutely modern," as Rimbaud once dreamed, but off-modern. A lateral move of the knight in game of chess. A detour into some unexplored potentialities of the modern project.

Broken-tech art doesn't thrive in destruction. At times, I go so far as to hit my computer, give it a mild spanking, push it to the limit. I want to handle it manually, like a craftsman handles his tools but without a craftsman's faith in the materials. Yet I never wish to annihilate the computer and return to the anxieties of leaking pens and inkblots on the grid-paper of my childhood. Broken-tech art is not Luddite but ludic. It challenges destruction with play.

Short Shadows, Endless Surfaces

In the early twentieth century French photographer Jacques-Henri Lartigue wanted to make photography do what it could not: capture movement. The blurs on the image are photographic errors, nostalgia for what photography could never be, longing for cinema. Yet photography should not become as garrulous as a film. It offers an elliptical narrative without a happy ending. Its fleeting narrative potentialities could never find their scriptwriters and producers. There would always be a cloud or two, a crack on the surface of the picture, a short shadow that evades the plot.

With his inimitable oblique lucidity Walter Benjamin wrote about the importance of short shadows. They are "no more than the sharp black edges at the feet of things, preparing to retreat silently, unnoticed, into their burrow, their secret being."[51] Short shadows speak of thresholds. They warn us against being too short-sighted or too long-winged. When we get too close to things, disrespecting their short shadows, we risk obliterating them, but if we let the shadows get too long we start to enjoy them for their own sake. Short shadows urge us to check the balance of nearness and distance, to trust neither those who speak of essences of things nor those who preach conspiratorial simulation.

Broken-tech art is an art of short shadows. It turns our attention to the surfaces, rims and thresholds. From my ten years of travels I have accumulated hundreds of photographs of windows, doors, facades, backyards, fences, arches, and sunsets in different cities all stored in plastic bags under my desk. I rephotograph the old snapshots with my digital camera and the sun of this other time and the other place casts new shadows on their once-glossy surfaces, along with stains of lemon tea and the fingerprints of indifferent friends. I try not to use the preprogrammed special effects of Photoshop: not because I believe in authenticity of craftsmanship, but because I distrust the conspiratorial belief in the universal simulation. I wish to learn from my own mistakes, let myself err. I carry the pictures into new physical environments, inhabit them again, occasionally deviating from the rules of exposure and focus.

At the same time I look for the ready-mades in the outside world, "natural" collages and ambiguous double exposures. My most misleading images are often "straight photographs." Nobody takes them for what they are, for we are burdened with an afterimage of suspicion.

Until recently we preserved a naive faith in photographic witnessing. We trusted the pictures to capture what Roland Barthes called "the being there" of things. For better or for worse, we no longer do. Now images appear to us as always already altered, a few pixels missing here and there, erased by some conspiratorial invisible hand. Moreover, we no longer analyze these mystifying images but resign ourselves to their pampering hypnosis. Broken-tech art reveals the degrees of our self-pixelization, lays bare hypnotic effects of our cynical reason.

Errands, Transits

We are surrounded by the anonymous buildings of our common modernity, a part of the other International Style not commemorated in masterpieces but inhabited in the outskirts of Warsaw, Petersburg, Berlin, Sarajevo, Bratislava, Zagreb, Sofia. These buildings, often indistinguishable from one another, even by me in my own photographs, compose an outmoded mass ornament of global culture. That is only at first glance, of course. If we look closer we see that no window, balcony, or white wall is alike. People in these anonymous dwelling places develop the most nuanced language of minor variations; they expose singular and unrepeatable out takes of their ordinary lives: a lace curtain half-raised, a dusty lampshade in the retro colors of the 1960s, a potted flower that knew better days, a piece of a risqué underwear hung on a string here and there. The inhabitants of these buildings dream of elsewhere, simultaneously homesick and sick of home. The satellite dishes spread out over the ruined balconies like desert flowers.

Hybrid Utopias, Avant-Garde Imaginary

Are utopias still possible? Or shall we return utopias to their origins—in art, not in life? I found on the Web images of Tatlin's studio and of Nabokov's butterflies and accidentally printed one on top of the other. The result reminded me of my Soviet science classes, where we studied the projects of socialist biology, particularly the work of Ivan Michurin, who endlessly cross-fertilized pears and apples. Many years later I accidentally cross-fertilized two different twentieth-century dreams and aesthetic utopias which are often opposed to one another: Tatlin's improbable flight of the avant-garde imagination and Nabokov's equally improbable artistic homecoming.

38, 39

Through the errors I confronted my own unrequited nostalgia. Returning to Leningrad in 1989, after a nine-year absence and immigration, I came upon my old house in ruins. Everything was in a sad state of disrepair: not only the neo-Baroque facade in the style of Russian Art Nouveau of the early twentieth century, but also the interior yard and the back staircase that led to our communal apartment. I stood numb in front of the ruins of this familiar place, but only when I pulled out my camera to take a picture did I discover a graffiti inscription—"death"—on a rusting pipe.

Once back in the United States, I attempted to print the image of my home ruin. My cheap printer ran out of black ink but when I hit it several times, it obligingly began pounding out its unconscious in deviational and unrepeatable psychedelic colors. Later I found out that they were making a film in my half-demolished yard about the absurdist poet Daniil Kharms, whose books were illustrated by Vladimir Tatlin. The film documented the end of the Russian avant-garde.

A Critic, an Amateur

If in the 1980s artists dreamed of becoming their own curators and borrowed from the theorists, now the theorists dream of becoming artists. Disappointed with their own disciplinary specialization, they immigrate into each other's territory. The lateral move again. Neither backward nor forward, but sideways. Amateurs' outtakes are no longer excluded but placed side-by-side with the non-outtakes. I don't know what to call them, for there is little agreement these days on what these non-outtakes are.

But the amateur's errands continue. An amateur, as Barthes understood it, is one who constantly unlearns and loves, not possessively, but tenderly, inconstantly, desperately. Grateful for every transient epiphany, an amateur is not greedy.

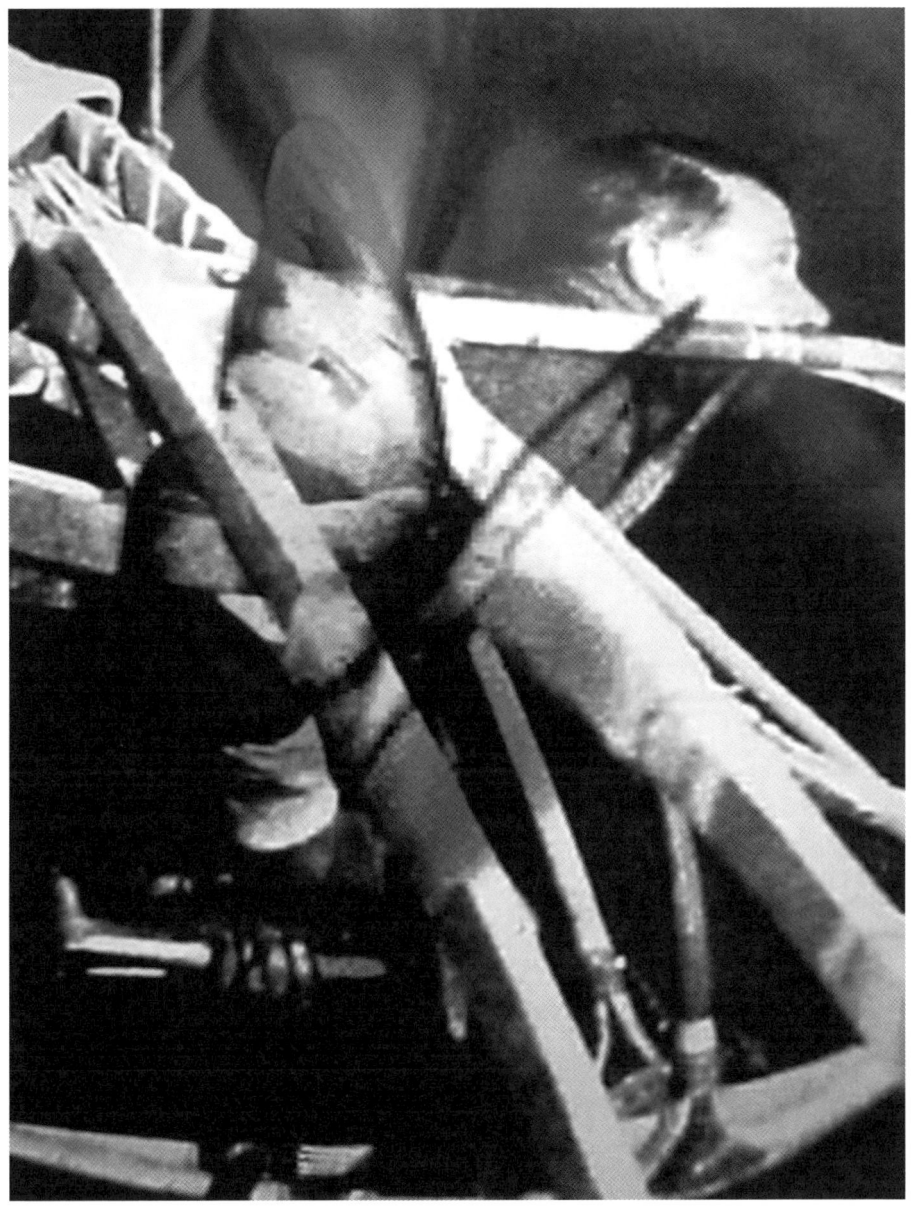

39 Svetlana Boym, Hybrid Utopias (Tatlin with Butterfly), 2002–7

Credits

1 Still from the film Tatlin's Tower, 1999, produced and directed by Takehiko Nagakura. Computer Graphics visualization by Andrzej Zarzycki, Takehiko Nagakura, Dan Brick and Mark Sich. Color altered by Svetlana Boym with permission of the filmmaker. Courtesy Takehiko Nagakura
4 The Tower of Babel, from Athanasius Kircher's Turris Babel, 1679. Courtesy Burke Library, Union Theological Seminary, New York
5 Natalia Verdi, Babylonian Tower, poster, from Moscou s'affiche, 1991. Courtesy Natalia Verdi
8 The second model of Tatlin's Tower at the International Exhibition of Decorative and Industrial Arts, Paris, 1925. Photograph: Alexander Rodchenko. © Estate of Alexander Rodchenko/ RAO, Moscow, VAGA, New York, NY
10 Letatlin exhibited in the Museum of State Art, Moscow, 1932. Courtesy Museum of State Art, Moscow
11 Fuselage of Letatlin, 1932. Courtesy Central State Archive of Literature and Art (TsGALI), Moscow
12 Vladimir Mayakovsky's catafalque in his funeral procession in Moscow, April 19, 1930. Courtesy Central State Archive of Literature and Art (TsGALI), Moscow
13 Alexander Rodchenko, Last Hour on the Lock, 1934. © Estate of Alexander Rodchenko/RAO, Moscow, VAGA, New York, NY
14 Work on Belomor Canal, 1930–33. Photographer unknown. Collection of Karelian State Regional Museum, Petrozavodsk
15 Vladimir Tatlin, White Jar and Potato, 1948–51. Courtesy Russian State Archive of Literature and Art, Moscow
16 Vladimir Tatlin, A Skull on an Open Book, 1948–53. Courtesy Russian State Archive of Literature and Art, Moscow
17 Vladimir Tatlin, color sketch for the set decoration of Chalice of Joy, 1949–50. Courtesy A.A. Bakhrushin State Central Theater Museum, Moscow
18 Vladimir Tatlin, color sketch for the set decoration of Chalice of Joy, 1949–50. Courtesy A.A. Bakhrushin State Central Theater Museum, Moscow
19 Boris Iofan, Vladimir Gelfreikh, Vladimir Schuko, and S. Merkulov, Palace of the Soviets, 1946. Courtesy Schusev State Museum of Architecture, Moscow
20 Model of Tatlin's Tower in the Musée National d'Art Moderne, Centre Georges Pompidou, Paris, 1979. Photograph: Hervé Lewandowski. Courtesy CNAC/MNAM/Dist. Réunion des Musées Nationaux/Art Resource, NY
21 Model of Tatlin's Tower in the exhibition "Der Traum vom Turm" (The Dream of the Tower) at Forum Kultur und Wirtschaft, Düsseldorf, 2004–05. © NRW-Forum, Düsseldorf
22 Model of Tatlin's Tower in the Moderna Museet, Stockholm. Courtesy Moderna Museet, Stockholm
23 Model of Tatlin's Tower in the New Tretyakov Gallery, Moscow, 1992–93. Courtesy New Tretyakov Gallery, National Museum of Russian Fine Art, Moscow
26 Constantin Boym, Palace of the Soviets and Tatlin's Tower, 1996. From the series Missing Monuments: Souvenirs for the End of the Century. Courtesy Boym Partners Inc.
27 Komar and Melamid, Temple, Exodus from Russia, performance on Mount Zion, Jerusalem, 1978. Courtesy Komar and Melamid
28 Igor Makarevich and Elena Elagina, Toadstool (with Tatlin's Tower), 2003. Courtesy XL Gallery, Moscow
29 Leonid Sokov, Mother and Child, 1986. Courtesy Leonid Sokov
30 Leonid Sokov, Watchtower, Self-Portrait as a Soldier, 1996. Courtesy Leonid Sokov
31 Ruins of a Gulag tower, 2005. Photograph: Irina Flige. Courtesy St. Petersburg Research and Information Center "Memorial" and Virtual Gulag Museum
32 Yuri Avvakumov, Perestroika Tower, 1990. Courtesy Yuri Avvakumov
33 Ilya and Emilia Kabakov, The Palace of Projects, 1995–2001. Installation at the 69th Regiment Armory, New York, 2000. Photograph: Gil Amiaga Foto Studio, Long Island. Courtesy Ilya and Emilia Kabakov and Public Art Fund, New York
34 Ilya and Emilia Kabakov, Building of "Contact with the Noosphere," Center for Cosmic Energy, 2000. Photograph: Igoris Markovas. Courtesy Ilya and Emilia Kabakov
35 Jane and Louise Wilson, Deck, Gorilla VI, A Free and Anonymous Monument, 2003. Courtesy Jane and Louise Wilson
36 Gordon Matta-Clark, Circus, 1978. © 2007 Estate of Gordon Matta-Clark/Artists Rights Society (ARS), New York
37 Robert Smithson, Entropic Landscape, 1970. © Estate of Robert Smithson/James Cohan Gallery, New York/VAGA, New York
38 Svetlana Boym, Hybrid Utopias (Tatlin with Butterfly), 2002–7. Courtesy Svetlana Boym
39 Svetlana Boym, Hybrid Utopias (Tatlin with Butterfly), 2002–7. Courtesy Svetlana Boym